THE
MORMON
WAY

Photographs/Text by
James A. Warner and Styne M. Slade

THE MORMON WAY

Prentice-Hall, Inc., Englewood Cliffs, N.J.

Design: Hal Siegel
Art Direction: Hal Siegel
Associate Designer: Rosemary Milewski
Production Editor: Dorothy Lachmann

Published in cooperation with Simon Communications

THE MORMON WAY,
Photographs/Text by
James A. Warner and Styne M. Slade

Printed in the United States of America

Prentice-Hall International, Inc., London
Prentice-Hall of Australia, Pty. Ltd., Sydney
Prentice-Hall of Canada, Ltd., Toronto
Prentice-Hall of India Private Ltd., New Delhi
Prentice-Hall of Japan, Inc., Tokyo

10 9 8 7 6 5 4 3 2 1

Library of Congress Cataloging in Publication Data

Warner, James A.
    The Mormon Way.

    1. Mormons and Mormonism–Pictorial works.
I. Slade, Styne M. II. Title.
BX8638.W37   289.3'3   76-7624
ISBN 0-13-601088-1

CONTENTS

Books by James A. Warner and Styne M. Slade

The Mormon Way
The Darker Brother

Also by James A. Warner

The Gentle People:
A Portrait of the Amish *(with Donald M. Denlinger)*

The Quiet Land
Songs That Made America

Acknowledgments

Many people have been
very kind and helpful to us
in creating this
book, and for that we
are grateful. Several of
them deserve acknowledgment:
K. Wayne and Ann Scott,
Bob Johnson,
Dorothy and Asahel Woodruff,
Jerry D. Harvey, Norm Bowen,
Wayne Smoot, Dee V. Halling,
and Keith Peterson.

THE
MORMON
WAY

INTRODUCTION

Sitting in the air terminal just outside Denver, Colorado, waiting for a flight to Salt Lake City, Utah, we could hear many different accents, both foreign and domestic. Some people were greeting other people whom they had known before at other times and places, some were seeking to become acquainted, and others were just waiting. The weather was anything but ideal for flying. Denver was experiencing a blizzard, and conditions were perfect for frayed nerves, yet no one was displaying them. Everyone was anxious to reach his destination, and so we sat, waiting for the tower to make a decision.

One thing we all had in common was that we were on our way to the April 1975 General Conference of The Church of Jesus Christ of Latter-day Saints. All saints who could make the trip were doing so, and though we were not saints, we too were going to the General Conference. For several months now we had been working on a picture book, taking the trip westward across the part of the United States over which Joseph Smith, Jr., and his successor Brigham Young led the early founders of The Church of Jesus Christ of Latter-day Saints almost 150 years ago.

The Church was first organized on April 6, 1830, in Fayette, New York. Its members are quite often called Mormons. Mormons are, in every sense of the word, Christians, but there are some differences that separate them from other Christian sects. Most of these differences are spelled out in the "Articles of Faith."

It all started when I was on my way to a library convention in Silver Spring, Maryland. I was driving along the Washington beltway; I rounded a curve, and there, in what seemed the very middle of the road, was a terribly impressive structure. I was convinced that I was seeing things. Hadn't I been along this road a short time before? It certainly hadn't been there then, had it? A day or so later, on my way home, I left the beltway and tried to find out more about this building. I was able to locate it, but because of all the construction I was unable to get close. That night on television I saw an explanation on the news. Jim had seen the news, too, and we thought perhaps it would be nice to take pictures, for the broadcaster had stated very clearly that once the building had been dedicated it would be closed forever to those not eligible for admission.

We went to Washington twice for open house. We took the tour and marveled, just as everyone else did, but two things really impressed both of us: first, the peace and contentment we seemed to see on most of the faces there, young and old alike, and, second, the crowds and the many different license tags, reflecting the distances that so many people had traveled to be there. We couldn't think of too much that either of us knew about Mormons. I knew that quite often young missionaries came knocking and that most times I was busy. I remembered, too, that many, many years earlier my brother-in-law had had a friend who was an "elder." Back home again, whenever I mentioned that I had gone to tour the temple, I was amazed at how little most people knew about the Mormon Church. Nevertheless, many people had stories and ideas about Mormons that were full of the kinds of errors and misconceptions that often surround strangers and different life styles.

Jim and I thought it would be nice to do a book about the Mormons, one that would introduce the reader to the impressive organization and people we had recently discovered and could see with new eyes. It would be primarily a picture book in which we would try to present highlights of both the Mormon heritage and of the lives of some Mormons of today whom we would meet on our journey of discovery.

Although The Church of Jesus Christ of Latter-day Saints is less than 150 years old, it already has a membership of more than 3½ million. By January 1976, it had more than 22,000 full-time missionaries and more than 6,000 additional part-time missionaries. There is no paid or professional clergy or ministry. Church offices are filled from the congregation, by people who have other jobs to support themselves. This church has few, if any, members on Federal welfare rolls because it has a workable welfare program of its own. I was impressed, and I am certain that our government could learn something by studying it. I've suggested this idea several times to Mormons, and they assure me that there is no magic formula; only real love of God, the Church and one's brothers provides the answer.

The Church of Jesus Christ of Latter-day Saints is perhaps the fastest-growing major church in the world today, and its president, Spencer W. Kimball, has called for members "to lengthen our stride," especially in family solidarity and in training a much larger and more effective missionary force.

This church had its origins in the eastern part of the United States, reached its maturity and fame in the western United States (particularly Utah) and has grown into a global church of unusual vigor and vitality—all because of a young boy, Joseph Smith, Jr., and his desire to find truth and wisdom.

9

The Articles of Faith

THE GODHEAD:1

  We believe in God, the Eternal Father, and in his son, Jesus Christ,
  and in the Holy Ghost.

RESPONSIBILITY FOR SIN:2

  We believe that men will be punished for their own sins, and not for
  Adam's transgression.

SALVATION: 3

  We believe that through the Atonement of Christ all mankind may be saved,
  by obedience to the laws and ordinances of the Gospel.

FIRST PRINCIPLES: 4

  We believe that the first principles and ordinances of the Gospel are:
  first, Faith in the Lord Jesus Christ; second, Repentance; third, Baptism
  by immersion for the remission of sins; fourth, Laying on of hands for the
  gift of the Holy Ghost.

AUTHORITY: 5

  We believe that a man must be called of God, by prophecy, and by the
  laying on of hands, by those who are in authority to preach the Gospel and
  administer in the ordinances thereof.

ORGANIZATION: 6

  We believe in the same organization that existed in the Primitive Church,
  viz., apostles, prophets, pastors, teachers, evangelists, etc.

SPIRITUAL GIFTS: 7

  We believe in the gift of tongues, prophecy, revelation, visions, healing,
  interpretation of tongues, etc.

SCRIPTURES: 8

We believe the Bible to be the word of God as far as it is translated correctly; we also believe the Book of Mormon to be the word of God.

REVELATION: 9

We believe all that God has revealed, all that He does now reveal, and we believe that He will yet reveal many great and important things pertaining to the Kingdom of God.

CHRIST'S REIGN ON EARTH: 10

We believe in the literal gathering of Israel and in the restoration of the Ten Tribes; that Zion will be built upon this (the American) continent; that Christ will reign personally upon the earth; and, that the earth will be renewed and receive its paradisiacal glory.

FREEDOM: 11

We claim the privilege of worshiping Almighty God according to the dictates of our own conscience, and allow all men the same privilege, let them worship how, where, or what they may.

OBEDIENCE TO LAW: 12

We believe in being subject to kings, presidents, rulers, and magistrates, in obeying, honoring, and sustaining the law.

SEARCH FOR TRUTH: THE GOOD LIFE: 13

We believe in being honest, true, chaste, benevolent, virtuous, and in doing good to all men; indeed, we may say that we follow the admonition of Paul— We believe all things, we hope all things, we have endured many things, and hope to be able to endure all things. If there is anything virtuous, lovely, or of good report or praiseworthy, we seek after these things.

—Joseph Smith

PART ONE THE

WAY WEST

Joseph Smith, Jr., was born in Sharon, Vermont. Why not start our journey there? We went to Sharon in the dead of winter, and just before we entered the town proper we began to see "beehive" markers. We were to learn that, by following the beehive emblem, we would find many Mormon places of interest all across the country. At one time the Mormons wanted to name the state of Utah Deseret. The word *deseret*, meaning "honeybee," is from the Book of Mormon, and is the symbol of industry and frugality.

Following these beehive markers, we climbed a very high hill to the birthplace of the prophet. There was a house, which had replaced the original Smith place, a large building suitable for meetings and perhaps some lodging, as well as a tall, slim, graceful monument to mark the place where the prophet had been born. The monument is 38.5 feet tall, one foot for each year that the prophet lived. Thirty-eight years are really a short lifetime in which to have accomplished all the things that he accomplished. We went inside and met a family visiting there. The family members spent time with us, telling us about Sharon, the prophet Joseph Smith and the Mormon religion. There is a rocking chair, beautifully crafted, some say by Joseph Smith himself; imagine my surprise to find that he, too, had learned the skills of carpentry.

Our next stop was Palmyra, New York. The Smith family had moved to this area while Joseph had still been very small. It was while he was quite young that he had had his first vision in the wooded area on his father's farm now known as the Sacred Grove. Not far from the grove is Hill Cumorah, the place where the angel Moroni instructed Joseph to find the gold plates, engraved in an ancient language; the translation of this text became the Book of Mormon. (The Book of Mormon does not replace the Bible; it complements it.)

The Book of Mormon was first printed in the town of Palmyra, and the building where this printing took place is still used daily as a variety store. Martin Harris, a friend of the prophet Joseph Smith, owned a very lovely home, and he mortgaged that home in order to pay for the original run of 5,000 copies. Today the Book of Mormon has been printed in more than twenty-four languages. Both the Peter Whitmer home in Fayette and the Martin Harris home in Palmyra are open daily to the public. They can be found by following the beehive markers. The original Martin Harris home was destroyed by fire. The man who held the mortgage and lived in the original house after foreclosure rebuilt on the same site.

I think the thing that still surprises me most is how new this church is, that today we can talk with members who can tell us so vividly how it was when their grandparents and great-grandparents literally walked across the country with handcarts to escape persecution for exercising the right to practice the religion of their choice, a right guaranteed in the American Bill of Rights.

It was at the farm belonging to Peter Whitmer that the Church was organized on April 6, 1830; the original log cabin is no longer there. David Whitmer (the son of Peter), Martin Harris and Oliver Cowdery were the three witnesses who testified to the world that they had actually seen the plates containing the text from which the Book of Mormon was translated. Oliver Cowdery was also most helpful in writing down what Joseph dictated.

Joseph Smith and Oliver Cowdery were baptized in the Susquehanna River at Harmony, Pennsylvania, now the town of Oakland. According to Joseph Smith, a heavenly messenger visited them and gave them instructions for baptizing each other after bestowing the Aaronic priesthood upon them. Not long after that "three other heavenly messengers, Peter, James and John, came as promised by John the Baptist. These ancient apostles of the Lord conferred upon Joseph Smith and Oliver Cowdery the Melchizedek priesthood and the keys of the Holy Apostleship, the same authority Peter, James and John had received anciently from the Savior."[1]

The Church was ever moving west because of opposition, persecutions and the like. The next stop was Kirtland, Ohio, where the very first temple was built. Kirtland is a quiet little town, about twenty miles east of Cleveland. The temple and the temple grounds are very restful and easy places to be. The lovely botanical gardens that surround the Kirtland Temple are said to preserve most of the original plantings.

From Ohio the Saints moved to Jackson County, Missouri, and later to Nauvoo, Illinois. During the winter of 1838-1839, Joseph Smith was in jail at Liberty, Missouri. The actual jail has been destroyed, but from its stones a new one has been erected to symbolize the cruelty that was unjustly inflicted upon Joseph. The massive door of the jail is authentic in size and structure and is shocking to see; the absence of windows is appalling. During his incarceration, Joseph received several revelations. He also spent time reading the Scriptures and sending warm, comforting letters to his wife, Emma.

The area that the Saints occupied in Nauvoo was originally swampland, and therefore no one else wanted it. Joseph and the Mormons were able to purchase this land at a fairly reasonable price. Right away they went to work and figured out a way to drain the area successfully; they proceeded to build a city much larger than Chicago. The word *Nauvoo* comes from the Hebrew and signifies beautiful location, "carrying with it also," says Joseph Smith, "the idea of rest." According to the *Nauvoo American Heritage*, during the brief period 1839-1846 the Mormons had

20 schools	3 coopers
one university	surveyors
a circulating library	brick masons
more than 2,000 well-built homes	plasterers

[1] Doyle and Randall Green, *Meet the Mormons* (Salt Lake City: Deseret, 1973).

35 general stores
14 boot and shoe stores
9 dressmaking and millinery
 shops
8 taylor [tailor] shops
13 physicians
9 law offices
3 newspapers
5 potteries
4 bakeries
4 stationers
6 blacksmith shops
7 wagon and carriage shops
5 livery stables
11 gristmills
3 soap and candle factories
3 match factories
7 brickyards
4 limestone kilns
3 lumberyards
2 ironmongers
straw factory
tanning mill
cabinetmaker
building contractors
comb factory
slaughterhouse

painters
glaziers
artisans
architects
3 notary publics
photographers
phrenologists
3 rope walkers
silversmiths
goldsmith
watch and clock maker
agricultural and manufacturing
 associations
Farmers Exchange
Carriage and Coach Association
5 horsebreeder and teamsters
 companies
3 glaze factories
opera
drama and 3 halls
water and power company--had
 started a dam to bring river
 traffic through the city, letting
 off and taking on at factories
 and businesses
cleaning and pressing shop
furniture factories⌡

Again the Mormons built a beautiful temple, which faced out over the mighty Mississippi River, and again trouble and persecutions stalked them. Joseph Smith was charged with treason. He turned himself in and was placed in a jail in Carthage, a town a few miles south and east of Nauvoo. His jailers were aware that the charges were false, and rather than place him behind bars, they permitted Joseph and some friends to occupy the upstairs quarters of the jail, a place reserved for jailers. Soon a mob gathered and surrounded the building. Some rushed past the guards and up the stairs, broke open the door and fired. Joseph, realizing that he didn't have a chance, turned to leap from the window; as he did so, he was hit by two bullets and fell out of the window to the ground below, near the well. The prophet had been brutally murdered. The official statement about the martyrdom in the *Doctrine and Covenants* was

To seal the testimony of this book and the Book of Mormon, we announce the martyrdom of Joseph Smith, the Prophet, and Hyrum Smith, the Patriarch. They were shot in Carthage jail on the 27th of June, 1844, about five o'clock p.m. by an armed mob—painted black—of from 150 to 200 persons. Hyrum was shot first and fell calmly, exclaiming: "I am a dead man!" Joseph leaped from the window and was shot dead in the attempt, exclaiming: "O Lord, my God!" They were both shot after they were dead in a brutal manner, and both received four balls.[2]

Perhaps it was the opinion of the persecutors that, once Joseph Smith was out of the way, the Mormon church would fall apart from lack of leadership, that this murder would mean the end of the Church and the saints, but, if so, they were mistaken. In Whittingham, Vermont, just a few miles south of where Joseph Smith was to be born, Abigail Howe Young had given birth to a son, Brigham, on June 1, 1801. When Brigham had reached adulthood, he had heard about, investigated and joined the Mormon Church. He had traveled across this country and Canada with and for the saints. When the prophet Joseph was murdered, the leadership of the church passed to Brigham Young. And what a man! With Brigham leading, the Mormons organized wagon trains and handcart teams and moved across the country under the most devastating conditions. The saints were headed west that time. Illnesses like cholera, typhoid fever and black scurvy accounted for many deaths. There are many different accounts of that western migration. One tells us that in the evenings, when members of a wagon train had set up camp and taken care of all the chores, the saints would sit around the campfire and sing praises to God, making such joyous sounds that once they frightened off a band of hostile Indians. The forward trains would plant food and feed for the oncoming trains, and they would leave messages along the way, saying "All is well."

Not all the stories have happy endings. Because of illness and hardship, many never reached the West. It is estimated that about 6,000 Mormons lie in unmarked graves along the way. In the town of Florence, Nebraska, there is a well-kept cemetery, where many are buried. Brigham Young was himself a sick man at the time the saints arrived in Emigration Canyon, the great salt basin that we know as Salt Lake City. As the Mormons descended from the mountains, Brigham recognized that they had reached their new home and declared, "This is the place."

Probably no other frontier builder worked under such trying conditions as did Brigham Young. He set up guidelines and made the following list of requirements for a family of five for the journey:

1 strong wagon
2 or 3 milch cows
2 or 3 good yoke of oxen, ages 6-10

[2] *Doctrine and Covenants* 135:1

1 or more good beeves
3 sheep, if can be obtained
1,000 lbs. of bread stuff in good sacks
1 bu. of beans
100 lbs. of sugar
1 good musket or rifle to each male over 12, 1 lb. powder, 4 lbs. lead
1 lb. of tea, 5 lbs. coffee
a few lbs. of dried beef or bacon
25 lbs. of seed grain
25 100-lb. farming and mechanical tools
clothing and bedding per family, not to exceed 500 lbs.
cooking utensils; bake kettle, fry pan, coffee pot, teakettle, tin cups, plates,
    forks, knives, spoons, pans, etc.
a few goods to trade with Indians
15 lbs. of iron and steel
a few pounds of wrought nails
1 gallon of alcohol
10 lbs. dried apples, 5 lbs. dried peaches
25 lbs. salt, 2 lbs. black pepper, 20 lbs. soap, 5 lbs. soda
1 lb. cayenne pepper, 1 lb. cinnamon, ½ lb. cloves, 1 doz. nutmegs
1 lb. mustard, a good tent, and furniture to each 2 families
1 or more sets of saw and gristmill irons to each 100 families
1 fish seine for each company, 4 or 5 hooks and lines
2 sets of pulley blocks and rope for crossing rivers to each company
2 ferry boats to each company, each wagon to carry one ton without people,
    or 2800 lbs. with them
10 extra teams per company of 100
N.B.—In addition to the above list, horse and mule teams can be used as well
    as oxen. Many items of comfort and convenience will suggest themselves to
    a wise and provident people, and can be laid in in season; but none should
    start without filling the original bill.

When the wagon trains were organized and Brigham had compiled the preceding list of requirements for families making the trek, last on the list were items of comfort and convenience. This was because they needed to take so many things and had so little space for them. However, Brigham strongly urged them to take anything and everything interesting and useful that could be used for educating, anything of a historical, geological, astrological background, maps and creative writings, as well as old text books. With these the very first school in the Salt Lake Valley was opened just three short months after the first wagon train arrived. Not only children but many adults became regular attendants of that early school. According to Clarissa Young Spencer, a daughter of Brigham Young, it was indeed an unusual school where languages such as Hebrew, Greek, German and even some Tahitian languages were taught. This was possible because of the missionaries having been in so many different areas of the world and possibly, too, because of the converts from those localities.[3] Brigham had had less than two weeks of actual schooling, but he knew the value of a good education. He founded the Deseret University, now the University of Utah, as well as Brigham Young University at Provo, Utah. He insisted on books and developing the arts. The Beehive House in Salt Lake City, Brigham's own home, is an example of the refinement that he insisted on. Imagine lace curtains and a lovely rosewood piano in the middle of the desert in the 1850s. There was an intercom system and a dumbwaiter. Brigham Young's home now is much as it was then.

Brigham Young was truly an exceptional man. He accomplished the almost impossible. It is said that he is the father of large-scale irrigation in the United States. Looking at the desert waste he saw the need for water, for agriculture had to be the basis of his community. At the first attempt at plowing, the saints found the ground hard, dry and unyielding. Several plows were broken in this attempt. Then, with Brigham Young's guidance a group of saints set about and put a dam in the creek and flooded the land. This was the beginning of the scientific systems now used in the rest of America and other parts of the world.

Although the Mormons had been told that nothing would grow in this hard ground of Utah, once the irrigation problem was settled, plant they did. In 1848, the second year, they planted corn and grain and had a good crop started. Just before harvesting time, a horde of crickets came and began to eat up everything. The Mormons didn't know what to do, and facing a new year without the harvest that they had so looked forward to was almost unbearable. Then a miracle happened—from out of nowhere came a flock of seagulls. They swooped down over the crops and simply ate the crickets one by one, leaving the crops intact. Today the seagull is the official bird of Utah, and to honor it, the Mormons have built a monument inscribed "In grateful remembrance of the mercy of God to the Mormon pioneers."

It is this same journey that Jim and I took, from Sharon, Vermont, to Salt Lake City— The Mormon Way.

19   [3] Clarissa Young Spencer and Mabel Harmer, *Brigham Young at Home* (Salt Lake City: Deseret Book Company, 1974).

Doubt not, but be believing,
and begin as in times of old, and come unto the
Lord with all your heart.

Book of Mormon 9:27

The beehive is a symbol widely used on historical markers or sites along the Mormon way. The Mormons originally named their intermountain empire Territory of Deseret, which means "Honeybee."

I the Lord knowing the calamity
which should come upon the inhabitants of the earth,
called upon my servant Joseph Smith, Jun., and spake
unto him from heaven, and gave him commandments.

Doctrine and Covenants 1:17

The monument marking Joseph
Smith's birthplace in Sharon, Vermont.

... and thou
shalt be missed, because thy seat will be empty.

1 Samuel 20:18

Joseph Smith's rocking chair.
This chair is believed by some to have been made
by Joseph Smith and is in his house
at Sharon, Vermont.

And the fame of this house
shall spread to foreign lands; and this is the
beginning of the blessing which shall be poured out
upon the heads of my people.

Doctrine and Covenants 110:10

The boyhood home of Joseph Smith
in Palmyra, New York. He was living here with his
family when he had the first visitation. The Sacred Grove
is just across the road on the same farm.

A young boy had an idea—
great events come by and through people having ideas—
and this boy had an idea that religious conflict was
never born of the Church of Jesus Christ. He knew
something was wrong somewhere; he knew that one
might be right, therefore all the others must be
wrong, or else they must all be wrong. And so in
the sincerity of his youth and with undaunted faith he
went to the only source from which anyone can
obtain wisdom pertaining to the gospel of Jesus Christ;
He went to God Himself.

Matthew Cowley

The Sacred Grove at Palmyra,
New York, where Joseph Smith had his first visitation.

Therefore
I will write and hide up the records in the earth.

Book of Mormon 8:4

Statue of the angel Moroni at Hill Cumorah.

The Gospel is indeed the plan
which the Creator of the universe has devised to guide
His children and bring them back to Him.

The Book that was the "record"
hidden at Hill Cumorah by Moroni.

The time of fulfillment is
in the unfathomable wisdom of the Lord. It is well to
teach all people to be prepared for the fulfillment of
prophecy and leave all else to Him.

The home of Martin Harris.

We are obligated to bear testimony ...
that in our hearts, by the revelation of the Holy Spirit
to our souls, we know of the truth and divinity of
the work and of the doctrines that we teach.

The Peter Whitmer farm.

For the gate by which
ye should enter is repentance and baptism by water....

The Susquehanna River at Harmony,
Pennsylvania, where Joseph Smith and Oliver Cowdery
baptized each other.

It is expedient in me that the first elders
of my church should receive their endowment from
on high in my house, which I have commanded
to be built unto my name in the land of Kirtland.

Doctrine and Covenants 105:33

The very first Mormon temple, Kirtland, Ohio.

Remember, we were also told
to dress the garden and keep it. Stewardship! It is one
of the loveliest words in our language. We must
develop a new tenderness toward the earth.

Helen Candland Stark

The Botanical Gardens around the Kirtland Temple.

O, God, where art thou?

Doctrine and Covenants 121:1

The prison door
at Liberty Jail, Jackson County, Missouri.

Thy days are known and thy years
shall not be numbered less; therefore, fear not what
man can do, for God shall be with you
forever and ever.

Doctrine and Covenants 122:9

A letter to Emma, Joseph Smith's wife.

The Constitution of the United States is a glorious standard; it is founded in the wisdom of God. It is a heavenly banner; it is to all those who are privileged with the sweets of liberty, like the cooling shades and refreshing waters of a great rock in a thirsty and weary land.

Joseph Smith, Jr.

The American flag outside a Mormon historical place. Mormons are most patriotic and support civil authority wherever they live.

The Lord has revealed in this day
the plan of salvation which is nothing more or less
than the way to the spiritual realm in character
worthy of entrance into His kingdom.

President David O. McKay

A tree in the swampland at Nauvoo, Illinois.
The land was so swampy when the Mormons first
arrived that they were able to purchase it at a low price.
Here the Mormons built the greatest city in the
West at that time.

True wealth consists in the skill
to produce conveniences and comforts from the
elements. All the power and dignity that wealth can
bestow is a mere shadow, the substance is found
in the bone and sinew of the toiling millions.
Well directed labor is the true power that supplies our
wants. It gives regal grandeur to potentates.

Brigham Young

Corn growing in the fields around Nauvoo
in what was once untillable swampland.

One important requirement
of a prophet is that God speaks through him.

A. Theodore Tuttle

The Joseph Smith house in Nauvoo,
which is not the property of the Church of Jesus Christ
of Latter-day Saints. A large restoration program is
now in progress in Nauvoo. Unfortunately the Joseph
Smith house has not been included in the project,
but it is open to tourists and is very impressive.

... the Lord appointed other seventy also,
and sent them two and two... into every city and
place, whither he himself would come.

Luke 10:1

This is a replica of the very first Seventies Hall.

The fullness of the earth is yours,
the beasts of the field, and the fowls of the air, and
that which climbeth upon the trees and walketh
upon the earth.... Yea, all things which come of the
earth are made for the benefit and the use of man.

Nauvoo became a fruitful,
healthy and prosperous town during the Mormon stay.

And had he been spared a martyred's fate till mature manhood and age, he was certainly endowed with powers and ability to have revolutionalized the world in many respects, and to have transmitted to a posterity a name associated with more brilliant and glorious acts than has yet fallen to the lot of mortal.

Parley Pratt

Carthage Jail, Carthage, Illinois.

The "martyr's window" at Carthage Jail,
from which Joseph Smith fell or hurled himself.

Persons who are successful as cultivated, compassionate beings may do more to change the world and contribute to humanity than all the world's leaders could hope to do. Peace begins in men's hearts. To be at peace with self and with God is a remarkable achievement, but to aid others, and one's children in particular, in reaching this end is the basis of true greatness.

Perry Datwyler

The bust of Brigham Young
on his grave in Salt Lake City.

And should we die before our journey's through,
Happy day! All is well!
We then are free from toil and sorrow too;
With the just we shall dwell.

William Clayton, "Come, Come, Ye Saints"

A wheel from a wagon
or handcart that helped to move the Mormons west.

Go and explore where you will,
and you will come back here every time and say
this is the right place.

Brigham Young

The monument at Emigration Canyon,
at the entrance to Salt Lake City. It was at this spot that
Brigham Young first viewed the valley and said,
"This is the place."

The most important of the Lord's work
you will ever do will be the work you do within
the walls of your own home.

President Harold B. Lee

Lace curtains in Brigham's house
are typical of the refinement that he strove for.
Grandness and finery were parts of the Mormon culture
in frontier days. This and the next picture show the
splendor that was sometimes attained.
Of course, all Mormon homes were not like this one,
but always there was a striving for betterment.

A home can be an earlier heaven. It often is.

Richard L. Evans

A guide in Brigham Young's house.
Note the rich velvets and woods.

The seagull monument
on the Temple grounds in Salt Lake City.

God moves
in a mysterious way, His wonders to perform.

A seagull in flight.

PART TWO THE

WAYS OF
MORMONS

My interest in the Mormon Church was magnified a thousand times after my first trip to the Washington Temple. I was impressed by it, by its Celestial Room and the baptismal font. They were evocative, offering a peaceful type of beauty. I was so moved that I had to sit for a moment to think about all my feelings, to savor all that I was experiencing.

I have visited the temple in Salt Lake City many times, but our Washington Temple was much more impressive to me at that time. I have since changed my mind. The Washington Temple is or is not the most majestic, but each of the temples has its own unique charm and loveliness. When I look at the Salt Lake City Temple at night, with all the lights on, it seems as if a thousand pearls are strung around its spires. When visiting the Washington Temple at night, the thing to see is the stained-glass windows up close, all lit up. What beauty!

The Mormons had opened the doors to share their newest temple with the world—to all who would come. Great pains had been taken to assure visitors' comfort, to answer all their questions, to share their joys; the only mention of money was an announcement that no contribution was expected. There is a visitors' center for those who want additional information. Imagine my amazement and irritation at hearing the misinformation that unthinking people often repeat! Now when I visit a Mormon temple, I have a fuller knowledge of all its functions.

The Mormon Tabernacle Choir is a natural successor to the saints' voices that were lifted in song all the way across the Middle West into Utah. They had sung to God for help, for guidance, for relaxation and for encouragement, from the time that they had started their wagon trains across the country toward their western homes. Today they sing to praise and thank God and to entertain and delight the world. The song "Come, Come, Ye Saints" was written during the western trek. The choir was first organized as early as 1847. I don't know how many members were in the original group, but today there are about 375 members, from all sorts of ethnic and economic backgrounds. There are husband-and-wife teams, bankers, secretaries, nurses and engineers, some of whom travel as much as 100 miles (170 miles in at least one instance) for weekly rehearsals. The choir has traveled all over the world singing. I have had a long love affair with this group, but then hasn't everybody? As far as I was concerned, the Mormon Tabernacle Choir was simply the name of the group. I never thought of it as belonging to a church or specific group of people. It belonged to everybody; it was ours, as American as apple pie. I can't imagine a Christmas season without the choir and its music.

We met a man who had the wonderful job of traveling with the choir. He told us many interesting things about the choir and its travels. One of its trips was to Salzburg, Austria, where the movie *The Sound of Music* was filmed. The bus driver was giving the choir a night sightseeing tour through the city streets, and as they returned to the hotel, suddenly the group began to sing, impromptu, "The Sound of Music." Imagine being on a bus at night in Salzburg with the Mormon Tabernacle Choir! I honestly don't believe that Richard Rodgers and Oscar Hammerstein could ever have heard their music sung more beautifully. What wouldn't I give to have heard that concert! I let my imagination run even farther. Imagine jetting to all these places around the world with this choir and hearing it practice! A giant silver bird, with the voices of the Mormon Tabernacle Choir....

While in Salt Lake City, we saw shelves upon shelves of genealogical records. Built into the side of the mountain just outside the city are the vaults, where additional records are kept. These records aid the members of the church in performing the ordinance work for the salvation of their dead in the temples of the Lord. As church members grasp the beauty and harmony of the temple ordinances they resolve deep in their hearts to live truer and finer lives. As families are forever, the Mormons are constantly updating these records and doing church work for many, family members and sometimes others, who died before they were able to avail themselves of temple benefits. These records do not include only Mormon families. My mother's family name is Binkley, and I went to the shelves to see if I could find any other members. Sure enough, there the family was; I found when the name Binkley first appeared in the United States, as far as records can determine. The genealogical records will be one of the very first sites I shall head for when I return to Salt Lake City.

The Mormon Church has one of the largest and most successful Boy Scout programs today, with one of the highest levels of participation anywhere in the world. We all know that the aims of the scouts are character development, citizenship training and personal fitness. These aims are also those of the Church, and scouting thus comes naturally to Mormons. At a recent scout affair, one of the Mormon elders, S. Dilworth Young, was addressing some scoutmasters; and along with other things that he shared with them, he said, "One of your greatest obligations is to teach in the environment of the out-of-doors, and that every grove can be a sacred grove, every mountaintop a Sinai where the boy may receive his revelations. Teach him how to know when these come."

"Relieving those who are able to but unwilling to work is ruinous to any community" are the words of Brigham Young. He also said, "It is a disgrace to every man and woman that has sense enough to live not to take care of their own relatives, their own poor, and plan for them to do something they are able to do." The Mormon Church has done something about its human family. In Salt Lake City there is Welfare Square, and there are other such places wherever you find Mormons.

We visited Welfare Square, which is completely staffed by volunteer workers. There was a large building housing a supermarket comparable in scale to any in the country. It was bulging with fresh produce, meats and dairy products—everything necessary to nourish a family. It was there that we first saw the famous Deseret labels, designating the Church brand, the brand money won't buy.

At one end of the building is a clothing store, and upstairs a shoe store. Great care has been taken to ensure that such items are packaged attractively, so that it will not be demeaning to shop there. There were volunteer craftsmen at work; we saw weavers working on rugs of the kind that we had noticed in quite a few houses undergoing restoration at Nauvoo.

All business transactions or exchanges are handled through an office marked "Bishop's Orders." This store not only provides all the necessities for a needy family's comfort, but it also provides jobs and volunteer work for those who have a need to give. And what responsible person doesn't?

The Relief Society was formed in 1842, twelve years after the Church was organized. It was organized to relieve the suffering of anybody who came. It has since branched out into other interesting projects, including the teaching of home skills and knowledge to all women members. One Relief Society project is the food-storage program. Mormons are instructed to maintain a year's supply of food for emergencies. So often they are accused of hoarding food, but that is far from the truth. Because emergencies can crop up at any time, they have merely adopted a sort of preparedness. After the hurricane in Honduras on September 19 and 20, 1974, the Mormons were a great source of emergency help. At the Relief Society women are also taught new ways to make their homes attractive, pleasant and wholesome places in which to rear families; nutrition and health are part of the program, as is awareness of different life styles and cultures. If the saints are indeed a world church, then what better way is there to learn about its various members around the world and to communicate with them than to show interest in what interests them and shapes their lives?

Mormon families are instructed to forgo coffee, tea, cola, and all other caffeinic beverages, as well as alcohol and tobacco. They emphasize nutritious food, exercise, hard work and a family-centered home life. Statistics seem to show that this emphasis results in longer lives and a substantially lower rate of cancer than are common among their non-Mormon fellow citizens.

I suppose that both curiosity and desire took me to our local Mormon chapel. I found a church just a few miles from my home, found out the schedule for services and attended. I was surprised at how many members I knew—one family living just three doors from me and another that I had taught Sunday School with twenty years earlier.

If one has never visited a Mormon church before, perhaps at first he will notice, as I did, the absence of the cross, the symbol that so often designates Christian churches. Mormons most definitely are Christians, but they explain that they exclude crosses because the cross symbolizes the death of Jesus Christ. The Mormons want us to know that Christ lives!

They say that we can judge the future of a church by the size of its younger congregation. Assembled at our local chapel was the youngest congregation that I have ever seen. Some of the children were quite audible, not necessarily crying but just making "I'm here, too" noises. When it was time to attend to the program, the children were still demanding to be heard, but no one seemed bothered; the speaker simply spoke above their voices, and in a short while I too was no longer aware of the competition. I did, however, mention it to the young man sitting next to me. His reply: "We want our children here with us. We feel if we don't have them here with us now, they won't want to be here with us later on."

A part of the service was a testimonial or inspirational talk given by a very young girl, only seven or eight years old. Mormon children are encouraged to speak before the entire congregation at a very early age. I think it gives them confidence to know that what they have to share, regardless of how much or how little, is appreciated and needed as much as they need to give it. Former Governor George Romney of Michigan, a Mormon, has said that he thinks that the Church has been the most important part of his own training, the part most responsible for his achievements.

The sacrament was passed by very young but efficient boys. It was most inspiring to see the young going about the order of the service in a most reverent way—the same children that I had seen playing an equally efficient game of baseball only a day or so before on the church grounds.

There was an announcement of a Penny Parade before we broke up into smaller groups to study. It is a fund-raising device by which healthy children give a penny for every year of their ages to the Primary Children's Hospital. In the future the funds will go to children needing medical assistance throughout the world. Mormon children are taught very young to have concern for those less fortunate than they.

Many times when I am preparing to go to my own church I feel a great need for a spiritual lift. Usually the lift that I receive at church will last a day or so, sometimes if I'm lucky a bit longer. Going to the Mormon chapel is an entirely different kind of experience. I receive the most subtle and delightful "soul feeding," which I hardly recognize at the time but which lasts the whole week. I'm always most anxious to go back. I feel that I have been among friends and family. I feel at home.

83

Once I was explaining to a friend that Jim and I were trying to put together a picture book about Mormons, and she asked me several questions: "Why the Mormons? Do *you* feel comfortable with them? Have you learned any of their secrets?" My answers to her were at some length.

First, why the Mormons? Because I had had the opportunity to tour the new Washington Temple and loved what I had seen there, both in the structure and in the people. I had been most fortunate in meeting the President of the Church, Spencer W. Kimball, and I wanted to know more about him and his Church. On the day that I first made the tour, a friend of mine in the Church made a very positive statement about death to a friend of his who was standing close by. At the time I was concerned about a member of my own family who was suffering a very nasty illness, which could be terminal; death was occupying a very prominent place in my thoughts. These two friends conducted a very comforting exchange. They were so relaxed and composed about the business of death and dying, expressing no morbidity, no painful sadness but only knowledge and acceptance that loved ones will be rejoined and with what rejoicing! I felt cheated that my own faith had never supplied this type of security, that death and dying are still quite painful for me to think about. Most Mormons aren't saddled with these feelings. I think perhaps that is because they know that families and marriages are not "till death do us part." They are eternal.

Second, did *I* feel comfortable with the Mormons? My friend did not add "because you are black," and perhaps I am taking it for granted that that is what she meant. My answer was a very positive "yes." I feel most comfortable with them. Before my visit to the church, I had felt that my Mormon friend was questioning my own Church and offering his as a replacement. I remember telling him quite smugly, "I don't feel unchurched, nor do I feel the need to look at other faiths and religions." That was before I had had the opportunity to visit his church. I now feel *more* at home in the Mormon Church and in Mormon company than I do in many other groups. Mormons offer one another brotherhood as no other group in my experience does. When you have a need, it is not necessary to ask for help; all you have to do is to make your need known, and help will be on the way.

During recent heavy rains a Church member's house started to leak. The leak very quickly turned into a gaping hole, and then the whole wall fell in, spreading water and dirt everywhere. The family called the church and told the bishop about the problem; quite soon enough members had assembled to repair the wall and to sweep out most of the dirt and water by nightfall—and they had fun doing it. The disaster gave them a chance to be brothers. On another occasion, a young friend in her fifth month of pregnancy was told by her doctor that she had to remain in bed until the baby was born. She had two preschoolers and was living more than 2,000 miles from her parents and relatives. The chances of obtaining paid help were slim. This young mother wasn't the least bit disturbed: She had sisters in the Church who would come in to take care of her and the children and to see that her family had hot meals daily. There was no need to telephone; she knew that they would come. Accepting these kind gestures carried no stigma. She would do the same and more for someone else should the need present itself, and she would welcome the opportunity to show her love and concern. President Kimball has said, and I am sure that he speaks for all Mormons, "When we are engaged in the service of our fellowmen, not only do our deeds assist them, but we put our own problems in a fresher perspective."[4]

Once, when some particularly unkind remark had been made about the Mormons' being a "bit clannish," my young friend said that perhaps it might be partly true. But I think that when a group has been censured and rejected by those who do not understand or approve of its religion and life, its members have a tendency to stay with those who share their ways and beliefs. In this way the chances of hurt feelings and misunderstanding are minimized.

Third, have I learned any Mormon secrets? What secrets? What I did learn is that the Mormons have no secrets. They are so anxious to share and to give what they have that they make everything available. There has never been a time when I have not been given a straightforward answer to a question. How can 3 million people keep a secret anyway? These people are so happy about their Church, and knowing that it is truly God's "restored" church on earth, they are most anxious that everyone else have the opportunity to know it also. They are bound by faith and committed to give all the information possible. Just recently they erected a new visitors' center in the heart of New York City. This and all the other visitors' centers (and there are many) are there to give out all the information anyone might seek. That is also the reason why there are so many young missionaries, traveling on bikes, in cars and on foot. These young men and women generally leave home at the age of nineteen years—an age when most young people are thinking about dating. They attend a brief week-long training period before they go out to share their "secret." Those going to a country where a different language might be a barrier spend a few weeks longer, taking a crash course at the language center at Brigham Young University. For the next two years (eighteen months for girls, who must have reached their twenty-first birthday), they must maintain themselves on money that they have worked for and saved, or they may perhaps be subsidized by their families. All young men are expected to go on missions. They must pay for their own room and board, car rental and whatever it takes to live. During this two-year period, they have a very rigorous schedule—walking, tracting, knocking on doors, trying to reach as many people as possible and to tell them about the Mormon Church and the many wonderful things it has to offer.

[4] Spencer W. Kimball, *The Miracle of Foregiveness* (Salt Lake City: Bookcraft, 1969).

They rise at an early hour and then must keep strict early-to-bed regulations, 10:30 p.m. for most. One day during the week, they have a half-day off to take care of their laundry, write home and carry out whatever acceptable activities they can manage to squeeze in. At 5:00 p.m. on that day, they are back on a work schedule. They are some of the nicest, most personable young men and women that one could hope to meet anywhere. During their mission period, they cannot attend "X" or "R" rated movies, date, go to parties, watch television or take part in contact sports. Their living quarters aren't always the most ideal, but they don't complain—not loud and long anyway. Imagine how terribly lonely this life must be for someone from a society in which the family is so closely knit and the center of life? Missionaries have much time to "ponder the Scriptures," and I think that is certainly partly responsible for their later building stable homes and treating their fellow men in more considerate ways. Quite often it is necessary for them to seek financial help from their families, which can put strain on the budget, but these loving families are proud of their "missionaries" and do whatever is necessary to help.

Baptizing is one of the duties of the young missionaries. Jim and I had the pleasure of watching our two favorites baptize and confirm a young woman. They were most serious and knowledgeable about what was expected of them, and they conducted the services in a most effective manner.

Going on a mission is not a privilege reserved exclusively for the young. I suppose that one could be called on a mission at any stage in his life. We met many adult couples in the mission fields who had raised their families, and quite a few had retired. I say "retired," but I am not too sure that this word is in the Mormon vocabulary. One has only to look at the ages of some of their presidents: David O. McKay was sustained as President of the Church April 9, 1951, at the age of seventy-seven years and served until his death at age ninety-six years. His period of service in the first Presidency and Council of Twelve was more than sixty-three years. Lorenzo Snow was sustained as President of the Church at age eighty-four years. Wilford Woodruff was sustained at age eighty-two years and died at age ninety-one years. But, retired or not, Mormons are asked to go on missions for two-year periods just as their young counterparts do. Several of these people have suffered really serious illnesses, yet all attest to having recovered and are truly grateful for the chance to serve on missions. Their radiant faces and dispositions do indeed confirm their pleasure.

So, with more than 28,000 missionaries in the field and efforts being made to double that number, Mormon "secrets" should surely get around!

When I had finished this long answer to my friend who had asked "Why the Mormons?" she said, "You know the trouble with these people is that they have made their Church and life so attractive, they don't want to investigate any other." Isn't that a beautiful unsolicited testimony?

Mormon families are quite different and special. A family begins with the temple marriage, one of the most important ordinances of the Church. Every family desires a temple marriage to bind it together "forever."

The Mormon woman is very feminine, supportive of her husband; demanding liberation just isn't part of what she is about. She is the mother and helpmate in the family and knows that her husband and children are working with her for the same goals: happiness and togetherness in this world and the next.

One of the nicest things that I would like to tell about is the family home evening. No doubt everyone has seen the bumper stickers that read "Happiness is family home evenings." One night a week, usually Monday evening, is set aside for the family to spend together praying, playing and working. It is all great fun. A time of family fellowship, this time is strictly reserved for being together.

Several times I have been invited to join family home evenings. Every family member must contribute something. Even my little friend Kim, not quite three years old, sang while her father played the guitar, and she helped her mother to serve refreshments that an older sister had made.

One family home evening that I was invited to was in the Utah prison, just outside Salt Lake City, part of a program carried on by the local wards. The inmates who wanted to participate had been assigned families. These assigned families brought their plans and games for the evening and held their home evenings inside the prison walls with their "adopted" family members from the prison rolls. Not only did this project bring each participating inmate news from the outside world, but it also let him know that people cared about him and would continue to be his family and to help him after his release. One of the reasons that we have so many repeaters in prisons today is that it is so difficult for released prisoners to find people who care, who will employ them and so on. The Mormon family will offer this type of help to the prisoner and will try to help him establish a meaningful life once he had paid his debt and been released. This help is offered with genuine concern and love and for no selfish reason. The statistics on rehabilitation of prisoners in the family home-evening project are dramatically better than those for released prisoners across the country. Couldn't our government learn something from the Mormon way?

With all the different problems plaguing our country today, it's quite clear to me that the Mormons do have some answers for a lot of things—welfare, prison reform, juvenile delinquency and a lower cancer rate (or, rather, generally better health), to name but a few. Our nation would do well to take a look, a serious look, at all that the Mormon Church has done and will do in the future. This Church and these people are dedicated to setting the world in order, and their world is our world. Whether or not we join them, we must look at them. They do have answers.

The present spiritual leader of the church is the Prophet Spencer W. Kimball, a grandson of one of the original twelve apostles under Joseph Smith. He was sustained as president on December 30, 1973, at the age of seventy-one years. He is a very dear man, and his very life seems a miracle. He had surgery for throat cancer in 1957 and, as a result, lost one vocal cord and half of the other. In 1972 he had open-heart surgery. He works very long and grueling hours, starting his day before the sun rises. Most men a third his age would find his schedule devastating. He has quite a remarkable record in church missionary work. Under his leadership, between 1965 and 1975, the rolls of full-time missionaries have risen from 12,600 to 22,000.

We had an opportunity to meet with him one afternoon in Salt Lake City. He had been in his office working, as usual, at a very early hour, and because his schedule was so tight, he elected to skip lunch to make time for us. We waited for him in a sort of foyer, and I thought that we would be shown into his office. But then an elevator door opened, and people got off. Suddenly all my senses and awareness told me that someone very special was there. I "felt" both his presence and his greatness. I will never forget that meeting.

President Kimball wants to double the number of missionaries in the field, and he wants so much to close the gaps in our relations with the American Indians, who have for so long been neglected. He wants to stretch hands across the world, to double, even triple, the inroads already made by the Mormon Church. Too often we tend to think of this overseas expansion as a recent program of the Church when actually it started many many years ago, almost as far back as the beginning of the Church. There are records of Mormon missionaries teaching and baptizing as early as the 1840's both in Europe and in the South Pacific, in places like New Zealand and Hawaii. When the missionaries originally set out for Europe, not only were they looking for new members but ones with particular skills and talents, people like engineers, cabinet makers and weavers, to name but a few.

The very first temple built outside the United States was the one in Hawaii, started early in the 1900's but because of World War I not completed until around 1920. When people become aware of how important the Temple is to Mormon families they can appreciate how necessary and vital it is to be geographically close to one. There are plans now to open three new temples in São Paulo, Brazil; Tokyo, Japan; and Seattle, Washington, where the number of Mormon converts is growing at an astonishing rate. Temples have already been established in Canada, England, Switzerland and New Zealand, and church growth is particularly strong in Asia, Australia, South America and the South Pacific. The church programs give particular attention and respect to unique life styles reflecting different cultural heritages. Many thousands have witnessed the marvelous programs that the Mormons sponsor at the Polynesian Cultural Center in Hawaii. There students of Brigham Young University—Hawaii Branch, formerly Church College of Hawaii, had developed programs to preserve the varied cultural heritage of Polynesia against the increasing presures of a modern tourist-oriented society.

The future for the Mormons appears to hold rapid growth in membership and increasing global expansion. In the United States the new Washington Temple has stimulated Mormon growth in the Eastern states, and the visitors' center opposite Lincoln Center in New York City is already baptizing many new converts a month.

From the very beginning Mormons have declared, "We are after truth, we commenced searching for it, and we are constantly in search of it, and so fast as we find any true principle revealed by any man, by God, or by holy angels, we embrace it and make it part of our religious creed."

Regardless of one's religious affiliation, the Mormon way certainly merits respect, admiration and even some personal examination.

The Church is true.
Keep its laws; attend its meetings; sustain its
leaders; accept its callings; get its recommendation
and enjoy its blessings.

Ezra Taft Benson

The Temple at Salt Lake City.

Where else in all the world
could you find such a well organized group,
such far reaching activities engaged in the building of
good citizens, furthering the work of the Lord,
and helping to bring to pass the immortality
and eternal life of man?

President N. Eldon Tanner

The new, modern Church office buildings
in Salt Lake City, with the Temple
in the background, showing the old and the new.

We believe that we have in this church the answers to all questions, for the Lord is the head of the Church, and He has given us the program. Our message is what it has always been, and our hope is that our people will live the commandments of the Lord. They have been revealed in the holy scriptures and by the living prophets throughout many years.

President Spencer W. Kimball

Statue of the angel Moroni on the Salt Lake City Temple.

God has given us no greater blessing
than that of belonging to a loving and loyal family—
and it will be so always and forever.

Richard L. Evans

A family listening to the April 1975 conference
as it is broadcast over loudspeakers in Temple Square,
Salt Lake City. In the background is a
sculpture of a family pulling a handcart on the trek west.

We are after the truth,
we commenced searching for it, and we are
constantly in search of it, and so fast as we find any
true principle revealed by any man, by God, or
by holy angels, we embrace it and make it part
of our religious creed.

President John Taylor

Presidents Kimball, Tanner and Romney
in the red velvet chairs at the April Conference
in Salt Lake City Tabernacle.

A celestial marriage is far more
to fight for and to live for, and to adjust for, than any
financial or other gain or beneficial arrangements
that two partners might have between them.

President Spencer W. Kimball

A bride and groom at temple.

As women of God,
filling high and responsible positions, performing
sacred duties ... women who stand not as dictators,
but as counselors to their husbands, and who, in
the purest, noblest sense of refined womanhood, are
truly helpmates ...we not only speak because we
have the right, but justice and humanity
demands we should.

Eliza R. Snow

At a meeting of the Relief Society,
another auxiliary arm of the Church.

The one persistent craving
of all humanity is for bread—spiritual and material.
But it is still up to the individual
to seek his own salvation.

L.H.O. Stobbe

Homemade wheat bread, honey and milk.
Food storage is taught as part of
the Relief Society program.

I sincerely believe if we do everything in our power to be obedient to the will of God, we and our families will never lack. If we are obedient as true followers of Christ and share what we have with those less fortunate than we, the Lord will keep his promise to watch over us and care for us. I will be glad that I have stores of food on hand so I can be of assistance to others. Perhaps like the widow who fed Elijah, the meal will then never fail in our barrels nor the oil ever fail in our cruses until prosperity comes again.

Theodore M. Burton

Home-canned tomatoes.

Welfare is for those
who have to give, as well as those who have not
to receive.

Vaughn J. Featherstone

Supermarket in Welfare Square, Salt Lake City.

Of course we may think we are thoughtful of parents and our older folk. Don't we send them gifts and messages on special days and anniversaries? And don't we make an occasional quick call as a token of our attention? It is something to be remembered on special occasions to be sure. But passing and perfunctory performances are not enough to keep loneliness in its place the whole year round. What they need in the loneliness of their older years is in part at least what we needed in the uncertain years of our youth: a sense of belonging, an assurance of being wanted, and the kindly ministrations of loving hearts and hands; not merely dutiful formality, not merely a room in a building, but room in someone's heart and life.

Richard Evans

An older woman at Welfare Square.

Let us make ourselves
capable of doing at least a little good and this will
occupy our minds upon something that is indeed
profitable to others and will divert our attention from
worshiping ourselves and blaming everybody that
does not do the same.

Brigham Young

A volunteer at Welfare Square, Salt Lake City.

In the days when the God of Heaven
shall comfort His people, and joy and gladness shall
be found among them, there shall be thanksgiving
and the voice of melody.

Alexander Schreiner
(adapted from Isaiah 51:3)

The choirmaster
leading the world famous Mormon Tabernacle Choir.

Let the saints be joyful in glory: let them sing aloud....

Psalms 149:5

The Mormon Tabernacle Choir "at home,"
with the large golden organ pipes in the background.

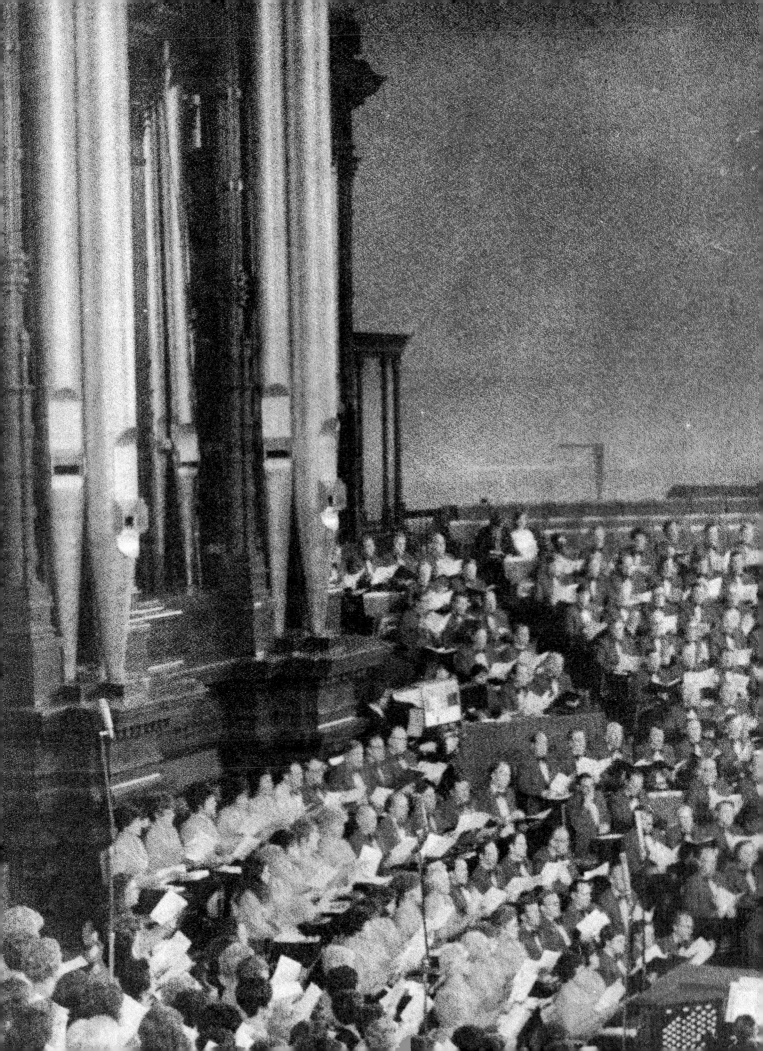

To each of us,
all of our ancestors are notable. We couldn't
get along without any one of them. By genealogical
work we identify with them and grow stronger in
our resolve to be worthy of the heritage left us by
their sacrifice and their nobility.

Dallin H. Oaks

Genealogical records and "seekers."

It is very important
that we help our boys set their goals high and then
set about to reach them.

President N. Eldon Tanner

Boy Scouts.
There are 224,027 Mormon boys in the Boy Scout
program, approximately 74,000 adult leaders and
14,344 units (1975 *Church Almanac*).

A mission
is not only a privilege and an opportunity, but a
solemn duty and obligation.

President Spencer W. Kimball

Missionaries greeting two young ladies
across from the information center at Lincoln Center,
New York City.

These ambassadors of the Lord Jesus Christ as they firmly believe themselves to be have trudged through mud and snow, swum rivers, and gone without common necessities of food, shelter and clothing in response to a call. Voluntarily fathers and sons have left homes, families and jobs to go to all parts of the world, enduring great physical hardship and unrelenting persecutions. Families have been left behind, often in dire straits, willingly laboring the harder to provide means for "their missionary." And through it all there has been a joy and satisfaction which has caused families at home to express gratitude for the special blessings received and missionaries to refer to this period as "the happiest time of my life."

Ezra Taft Benson

Missionaries walking
through a snow-covered field to visit a rural home.

America is a great and glorious land.
It is choice above all other lands. It has a tragic and
bloody past but could have a glorious peaceful future
if the inhabitants would really learn to serve God.
It was consecrated as a land of promise to
the people of the Americas...

President Spencer W. Kimball

Missionaries visit a picnic of the
National Association for the Advancement
of Colored People (N.A.A.C.P.).

Tell the sisters to go forth and
discharge their duties in humility and faithfulness
and the spirit of God will rest upon them,
and they will be blest in their labor. Let them seek for
wisdom instead of power and they will have all
the power they have wisdom to exercise.

Eliza R. Snow

Two girl missionaries
at Liberty Jail, Jackson County, Missouri.

Every boy and many girls and couples should serve missions. Every prospective missionary should prepare morally, spiritually, mentally, and financially all of his life in order to serve faithfully, efficiently and well in the great program of missionary work.

President Spencer W. Kimball

Missionaries staff
Mormon historical sites and visitor centers.

And now if your joy
will be great with one soul that you have brought
unto me... how great will be your joy if you should
bring many souls unto me.

Doctrine and Covenants 18:16

Baptism out of doors.

May we always remember
and acknowledge that Jesus Christ, the Son of God,
the Savior of the world, came and gave His life for
you and me, and accept his teachings as the way
of life and salvation and be prepared to so live that we
may be found worthy of his sacrifice as we prepare
ourselves to enjoy immortality and eternal life.
As we do this, we will bring glory to His name and
salvation to ourselves.

President N. Eldon Tanner

A baptism.

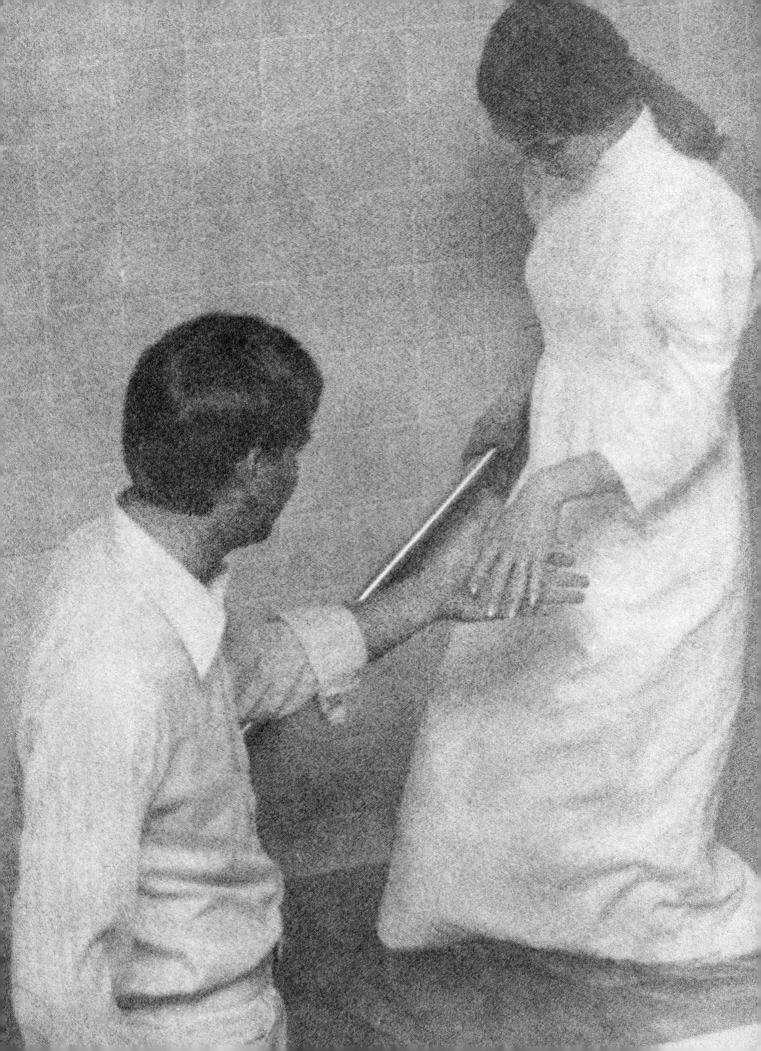

Happy homes give
to their inhabitants a taste of heaven on earth;
acceptance of the divinity of Christ's mission and
compliance with the principles of His gospel give
assurance of immortality and eternal life.

President David O. McKay

A mother and child.

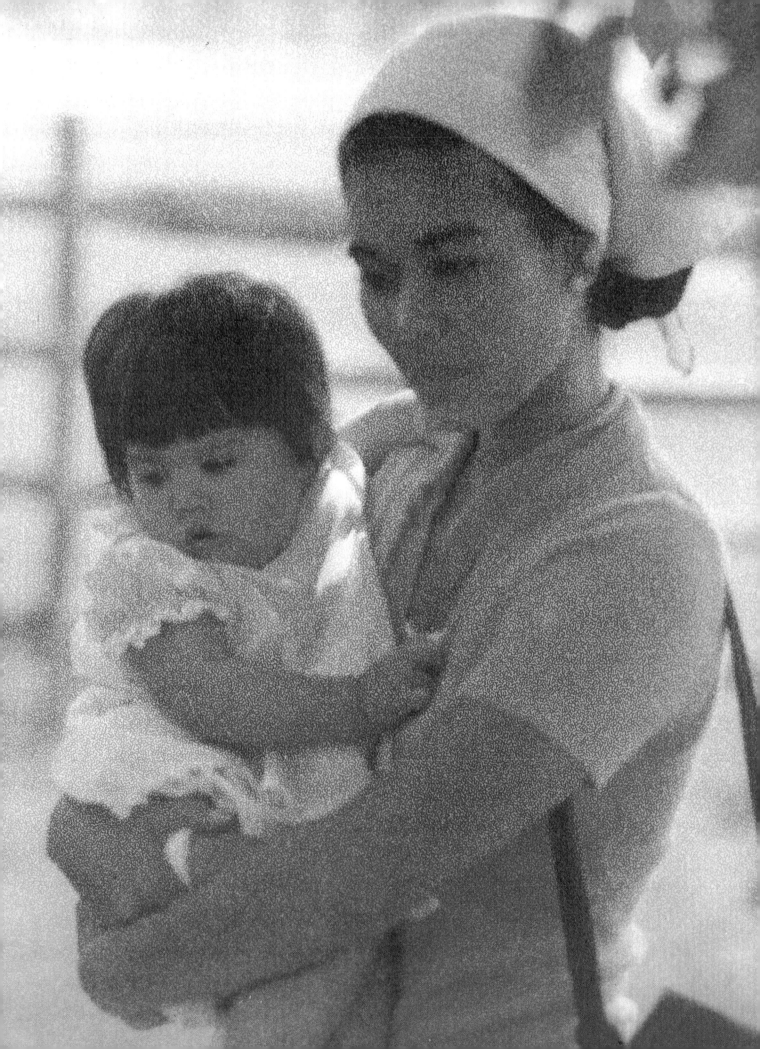

With our concept
of universal brotherhood it is untenable that we as a
people should entertain prejudice and ill will
against any of our Father's children.

LeGrand Richards

A Mormon in front of the Salt Lake City Temple.

The Lord has placed
the emphasis for real joy squarely on the family.

Hartman Rector, Jr.

A mother and baby.

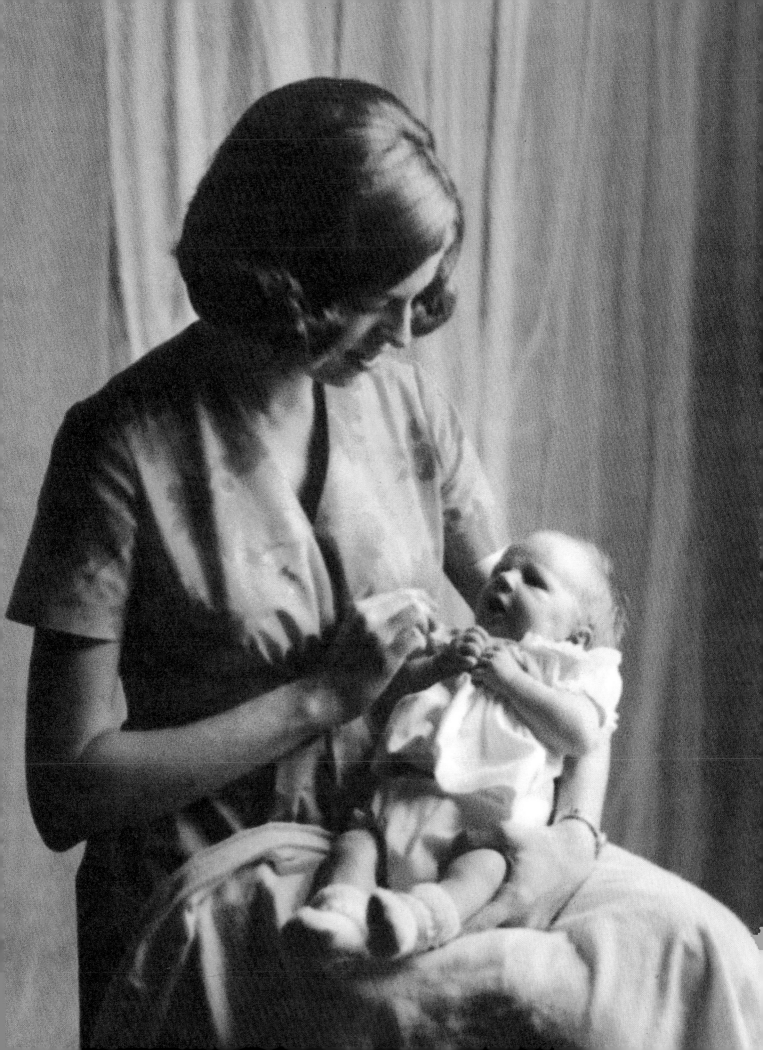

Here is the answer to the world's needs:
righteous, teaching parents, obedient, loving children,
faithfulness to family duties.

President Spencer W. Kimball

The family at play.

I believe that almost any woman
can become an outstanding wife and mother
if she will take advantage of the opportunities the
Church provides for personal development and
consistently apply the principles taught to us by the
Church concerning the building of a happy,
successful home.

Out of the corner of Mother's watchful eye.

The primary function of a Latter-day saint home is to insure that every member of the family works to create the climate and conditions in which all can grow toward perfection. For parents, this requires a dedication of time and energy far beyond the mere providing of their children's physical needs. For children, this means controlling the natural tendency toward selfishness.

President Harold B. Lee

A family outing in the snow in Sharon, Vermont. In the background is the monument marking Joseph Smith's birthplace.

The Latter-day saint wants his home
to be the setting for glorious family living, where love,
goodwill, and creative working together develop an
eternal bond between parent and child.

James A. Cullimore

Weekend family fun.

Society without basic family life
is without foundation and will disintegrate
into nothingness.

President Spencer W. Kimball

A family working together.

Thank the Lord for all the glorious
things He does; proclaim them to the nations.

Psalms 105:1

A Mormon farm.

Our primary purpose was to set up, insofar as it might be possible, a system under which the curse of idleness would be done away with, the evils of a dole abolished, and independence, industry, thrift, and self-respect be once more established amongst our people. The aim of the Church is to help the people to help themselves. Work is to be re-enthroned as the ruling principle of the lives of our Church membership.

Statement from the office of the 1st Presidency, October 1936

Bountiful, Maryland—Mormon co-op dairy farm.

The great love your parents have for you....
They loved you even before you were born. When
you finally came to them from your heavenly home,
you brought them a great joy that you will feel
someday, too, when you become fathers and mothers.
Your parents' love increases as you grow, and their
love for you will never cease.

President N. Eldon Tanner

Finger plays.

One of the gifts of a loving family
is the encouragement and confidence we receive
to magnify ourselves.

L. Tom Perry

Mother and teen-age daughter.

The constant exercise of our faith ...
is just as essential to spiritual health as physical
exercise is to the health of the body.

O. Leslie Stone

A female track runner at Brigham Young University.

Members are encouraged to seek learning from all good books and from any source. For is there anything virtuous, lovely or of good report or praiseworthy, we seek after these things.

There are other reasons why it is important for our young women to receive a proper education. Education is more than vocational. Education should improve our minds, strengthen our bodies, heighten our cultural awareness, and increase our spirituality. It should prepare us for greater service to the human family.

Dallin H. Oaks

The violin player.

Meditation
is the venturing of the soul into the unknown.
But it can be learned by anyone who has the courage
to think for himself. A likely initiation to meditation
is to ponder the scriptures.

Chauncey C. Riddle

In the shadows of the Washington Temple.

Of all mortal men,
we should keep our eyes fixed on the captain,
the prophet, seer, and revelator, and President of the
Church of Jesus Christ of Latter-day Saints. This is the
man who stands closest to the fountain of living waters.
There are some heavenly instructions for us that we
can only receive through the prophet.

President Ezra Taft Benson

President Spencer W. Kimball

When we realize the vastness, the richness, the glory of that "all" which the Lord promises to bestow upon his faithful, it is worth all it costs in patience, faith, sacrifice, sweat and tears. The blessings of eternity contemplated in this "all" bring men immortality and everlasting life, eternal growth, divine leadership, eternal increase, perfection, and with it all, godhead.

President Spencer W. Kimball

The Washington Temple at night.

GLOSSARY

ARTICLES OF FAITH: A simple, comprehensive declaration of the doctrines of the Church, first given by inspiration, accepted by the members of the Church as a standard of belief.

BISHOP'S ORDERS: 1. "Orders from the Bishop," with which, instead of cash, "customers" make "purchases" at Church Welfare Plan stores. 2. The sign which hangs over the check-out counter at Church Welfare stores.

CELESTIAL ROOM: The room in a Mormon temple used for meditation, the name suggesting the beautiful life to come.

DESERET: From the Book of Mormon, "honeybee," symbolizing industry and frugality.

DOCTRINE AND COVENANTS: A volume of Latter-day scripture which contains selections from the revelations given to Joseph Smith and his successors.

ELDERS: Ministers of Christ.

FIRST PRESIDENCY: The office of supreme directing power and authority over the Church.

HILL CUMORAH: Near the town of Palmyra in Manchester County, New York, the hill where the angel Moroni hid the gold plates from which the Book of Mormon was translated.

HOLY APOSTLESHIP: The office bearing the responsibility of carrying the gospel to all the world. One holding it knows of the divinity of the Savior by personal revelation.

LATTER-DAY SAINTS: People adhering to the religion of the Church of Jesus Christ of Latter-day Saints, often called "Mormons."

172

MORONI: The angel that appeared to Joseph Smith, told him that he was a messenger from God, and instructed him to find the gold plates that when translated became the Book of Mormon.

NAUVOO: From the Hebrew, "beautiful location," also carrying with it the idea of rest.

PRIESTHOOD: The order of men presiding as Church authorities, including two subdivisions, the Melchizedek (or Higher) and the Aaronic Priesthoods. The Melchizedek Priesthood is further divided into the elders, seventies, and high priests; the Aaronic, into deacons, teachers, and priests.

PROPHET: The spiritual head of the Church, from the word meaning teacher, revealer, or witness to the truth.

RECOMMENDS: Certificates issued by the Church to identify members and to certify their worthiness to receive certain blessings.

SACRED GROVE: The wooded area that the Smith family owned in Manchester County, New York, where Joseph Smith prayed for the wisdom to know which faith he should follow and was granted a revelation.

SEVENTIES: An auxiliary group of the Church with the specific duty to carry out missionary work throughout the world.

SUSTAIN: To give common consent; to give a supporting or affirmative vote to a candidate for president of the Church.

WELFARE SQUARE: A complex of buildings in Salt Lake City manned by volunteers where persons in need may get supplies such as food, clothing, furniture, etc.

173